THE MOTHER LODE OF LAUGHS!

What do you call a hooker with a runny nose?

Full.

―――――――

Did you hear about the Polish gambler?

He took a roll of toilet paper to a crap game.

―――――――

Why don't Italians have freckles?

They slide off.

―――――――

What do Arabian men do on weekends?

They lounge under palm trees and eat their dates.

―――――――

Why don't blind people go skydiving?

It scares the shit out of their dogs.

BOOK YOUR PLACE ON OUR WEBSITE AND MAKE THE READING CONNECTION!

We've created a customized website just for our very special readers, where you can get the inside scoop on everything that's going on with Zebra, Pinnacle and Kensington books.

When you come online, you'll have the exciting opportunity to:

- View covers of upcoming books
- Read sample chapters
- Learn about our future publishing schedule (listed by publication month *and author*)
- Find out when your favorite authors will be visiting a city near you
- Search for and order backlist books from our online catalog
- Check out author bios and background information
- Send e-mail to your favorite authors
- Meet the Kensington staff online
- Join us in weekly chats with authors, readers and other guests
- Get writing guidelines
- AND MUCH MORE!

**Visit our website at
http://www.zebrabooks.com**

STILL JOKING OFF

Johnny Lyons

Zebra Books
Kensington Publishing Corp.

http://www.zebrabooks.com

ZEBRA BOOKS are published by

Kensington Publishing Corp.
850 Third Avenue
New York, NY 10022

Copyright © 1999 by Johnny Lyons

All rights reserved. No part of this book may be reproduced in any form or by any means without the prior written consent of the Publisher, excepting brief quotes used in reviews.

If you purchased this book without a cover you should be aware that this book is stolen property. It was reported as "unsold and destroyed" to the Publisher and neither the Author nor the Publisher has received any payment for this "stripped book."

Zebra and the Z logo Reg. U.S. Pat. & TM Off.

First Printing: June, 1999
10 9 8 7 6 5 4 3 2 1

Printed in the United States of America

TABLE OF CONTENTS

Part One:	Sex, Drugs, & Rock 'n' Roll	7
Part Two:	Politics	19
Part Three:	Food Jokes	33
Part Four:	Hollyweird!	43
Part Five:	Ethnic Jokes	51
	Black Jokes	53
	Polish Jokes	59
	Hispanic Jokes	67
	Jewish Jokes	71
	Italian Jokes	77
	Gay Jokes	81
	Miscellaneous Ethnic Jokes	89
Part Six:	Very Sick Jokes	99

Part One

SEX, DRUGS, & ROCK 'N' ROLL

The magic four-letter word in any marriage is OURS!

Most women think that too many men know all about financial values but know nothing about human values!

The unfortunate thing about having visitors when you're a newlywed is they usually annoy you when you're young and busy. Do you think they'll come back when you're old and lonely?

Boy: What's your favorite subject?
Girl: Poetry.
Boy: Well, maybe you can help me straighten out my Longfellow.

What do you call a hooker with a runny nose?

Full!

What do you do with an elephant with three balls?

Walk him, and pitch to the giraffe!

The first night, Joe walks into a bar and says, "Bartender, give me a double." The bartender says, "Joe, what's going on? You don't drink." Joe says, "Yes, but I just found out my brother is gay."

The second night Joe walks into the her and asks for two doubles, hold the rocks. Bartender says, "Joe, what's happening? Last night a double, tonight two?" Joe said, "I just found out my other brother is gay, also."

The third night Joe goes into the bar, and says, "Bartender, give me a bottle of Scotch, and don't even talk to me until it's finished." The bartender says, "My God, Joe, aren't there any left who like women?" Joe goes, "Of course, my sister."

Things are so bad that a guy who calls his doctor and is told, "I'm sorry, you have herpes," says "Thank you so much!"

What's the definition of a bachelor?

A perverse son of a bitch who is depriving some woman of her God-given right to alimony!

A British commander is welcoming Smyth, a new recruit, to a remote outpost in India. "Don't worry about the dismal appearance here, Smyth. We manage to have a wonderful time. Let's see, today's Wednesday, so tonight's our boozing event. We bring in cases of beer, wine, and liquor, and get totally wasted."

Smyth says, "I'm very sorry, sir, but I got sick on alcohol when I was fourteen and haven't been able to touch the stuff since."

"Oh, don't worry," says the commander. "Tomorrow, Thursday, is a fabulous wenching event. We bring in two or three hookers for every soldier and have an absolute orgy."

"Oh no, sir, I couldn't do that," replied Smyth. "I got too much respect for me mother and me sister to ever do something like that."

"Smyth," the commander questions, "I don't like to be so blunt, but you don't happen to be a homosexual?"

"Absolutely not," explains Smyth.

"Pity," said the commander. "I guess you won't enjoy Friday night, either."

How can you tell a bachelor from a married man?

A bachelor comes to work from a different direction each morning.

A young, attractive man picked up his blind date and took her to a carnival. He asked her what she would like to do. She replied, "I want to get weighed." He obliged and took her to the weighing booth and happily won a prize for her. Then he took her on the ferris wheel and again, he asked her what she would like to do. Again she responded, "I want to get weighed." He refused to oblige her a second time.

Well, when she became indignant he promptly returned her to her home. When her roommate opened the door, she asked how her evening was. She said, "Wousy."

A married couple was invited to a costume party at the home of a neighbor. They decided to go as a cow, with the man being the front of the cow and the lady being the rear. They decided to cross the meadow between their house and the house where the party was to take place. Halfway across the meadow, the man said, "Honey, don't look now, but here comes a bull."

The lady said, "Oh my God, what will we do?"

The man said, "Well, I'm going to bend over and eat a little grass. I suggest you brace yourself."

A man and his wife were at the zoo one day, and they came upon a cage with an enormous male gorilla. The man asked his wife if she'd like to try something. He said, "Honey, do me a favor. Start to take off your clothes in front of that gorilla, and see if it becomes sexually excited."

She said, "Are you crazy? I'm not going to do that."

He kept asking and begging and finally, she thought it would be interesting to see if it would bother the gorilla. As she started to undress, the gorilla started to pound on his chest and swing from the roof, and the more she took off, the more the gorilla went crazy. The gorilla was now a raving maniac. And with that, her husband ripped open the cage door, threw his wife in and said, "Now tell him you have a headache."

What's the difference between a woman jogger and a sewing machine?

A sewing machine only has one bobbin.

Bob was a poor boy from the hill country. He was born with a strange birth defect: his feet stank. Bob's feet stank so badly that people shunned him. He grew up with no friends. He finally did land a job and began to see a doctor about his problem. The doctor treated him for an extended period but eventually had to tell Bob that medical science had no cure for his problem, and that he would have to live with it. Bob was so despondent that he went to the local bar and began to drink.

Shirley was also born in the hill country, not far from Bob. She too had a serious problem: she had the world's worst case of halitosis. Once Shirley landed a job she also began medical treatment but her problem did not respond to treatment and she became despondent.

Through sheer coincidence, Bob and Shirley found themselves at the same bar. Their eyes met across the bar and soon they were sitting next to each other. Bob managed to keep his feet pointed away from Shirley and Shirley managed to carry on a conversation without breathing directly in Bob's face.

The evening went well and they decided to go to a hotel together. As soon as Bob entered the room he went directly to the bathroom, took off his shoes and socks, scrubbed his feet as clean as they had ever been. Then he rolled his socks up in a towel and hid them under the sink. Shirley was next in the bathroom. She brushed her teeth, rinsed her mouth and she prayed. Shirley found Bob in the bed with his feet wrapped up in the sheets. She took a deep breath, lowered herself down on Bob's chest, looked him in the eye and said, "Before we do this, I have a confession to make."

Bob, shrinking back, said, "Oh, don't bother, I know. You ate my socks."

An altar boy at a Catholic church is told by the parish priest to refill the holy water fountain at the rear of the church. A few minutes later the altar boy comes running into the rectory excited and he goes, "Father, I just saw the most amazing thing happen by the holy water fountain."

"What happened?" asks the priest.

"Well, Father, this man came into the church on crutches. He went over to the holy water fountain and he blessed himself with his right hand, then he threw his right crutch away. Then he blessed himself with his left hand and he threw his left crutch away.

The priest says, "Oh my God, you've just witnessed a miracle! Quick, take me to him immediately."

"Sure, Father. He's flat on his back in the rear of the church."

Two farm boys from the country are on their first airplane ride across the ocean. Not long after takeoff the captain comes on the public address system. "Ladies and gentlemen, this is the captain speaking. I'm afraid one of our engines has failed. There's no cause for alarm since we have three other perfectly good engines. However, we will lose a little bit of speed and we expect to land at our destination one hour later than originally planned." The two lads look at each other apprehensively, but accept the news with good grace since no one else seems concerned. An hour later the p.a. system once again breaks the silence. "Ladies and gentlemen, this is your captain. This is a most unusual situation. A second engine has failed. Please stay calm and be patient. We have descended a bit and have lost more speed but we will continue on to our destination, although we will be an additional two hours behind schedule." The two hicks squirm uncomfortably in their seats but still say nothing. An hour later the captain alerts the passengers, "Ladies and gentlemen, this is the captain. We have declared an emergency as we have lost one of the two remaining engines. We are apparently making little headway but we are still flying. The flight attendant will pass out free drinks, and with a little bit of luck, we will land at our destination about six hours late."

Finally one of the country boys looks over to the other and says, "Gee, I hope we don't lose that other engine or we'll be up here all day."

How many graduate students does it take to change a lightbulb?

One, but it will take him seven years.

Ah, marital bliss. Sally and Irving are in bed. "Listen, Sally," says Irving, "do me a favor, and please close the window. It's cold outside."
"And if I close the window, will it be warm outside?"

A drunk was walking down the street with one foot on the curb and one foot in the gutter. A cop stopped him and said, "I've got to take you in—you're totally drunk."
The guy said, "Officer, are you absolutely sure I'm drunk?"
The officer said, "Yes, you're drunk."
The drunk says, "Thank goodness, I thought I was a cripple!"

The good priest Ronald O'Sullivan called on his old friend Rabbi Schwartz, in a terribly aggravated state. "Rabbi!" he yelled. "You've got to help me! I have to hear confessions in thirty minutes, and in one hour I have to be several miles away from the church to attend a funeral. Would you be kind enough to hear confession in my absence?"
The rabbi was shocked!
The priest said, "It's easy. Come on down to the church and I'll start hearing confessions, and you'll listen to exactly what I tell the parishioners." When they got to the church the priest sat in the confessional, and the rabbi sat in a hidden room next to the priest.
At first an apparently young woman came in and confessed, "Forgive me, Father, for I have sinned."

The priest said, "What have you done my child?"

"I have had sex with a married man!"

"How many times?" the Father asked.

"Four times, Father, and I sincerely regret this act of adultery."

The Father said, "For your penance say forty 'Our Fathers' and put $2 in the poor box, and you'll be absolved."

Then, another woman confessed that she had sinned, and made love to her daughter's boyfriend twice, The Father said, "Say twenty, 'Our Fathers,' and put $1 in the poor box, and you will be absolved." As soon as the woman left, the priest whispered to the rabbi that he could take over now, as he had to go to the funeral. The rabbi said fine; he thought he had a feel for hearing confessions, and authorizing penance.

The rabbi sat in the priest's chair, and another woman came in and said, "Forgive me, Father, for I have sinned by having sex out of wedlock." The rabbi asked how many times she had done this.

"Just once, Father."

"Well," the rabbi said, "you better go do it again!"

The woman said, "Do it again?!"

The rabbi said, "Sure, it's two for a buck!"

Did you hear about the girl who was dating a tractor salesman? They broke up, and she wrote him a John Deere letter!

According to the PTL, what is the eleventh commandment?

Thou shalt not use thy rod on thy staff!

Why did the bald man like to have holes in his pockets?

Because he liked to run his fingers through his hair!

A midget was accused of a rape in front of a judge. The judge asked the midget, "Did you do it?"

The midget responded, "Yes, but my friends put me up to it."

Part Two

POLITICS

COMMUNISM: You have two milk cows. The government takes both, milks them, keeps the milk and gives you half a pint.

———————

SOCIALISM: The government takes one of your cows and gives it to a neighbor.

———————

FASCISM: The government takes both cows and shoots one of them.

———————

NAZISM: The government takes both cows and shoots you.

———————

CAPITALISM: You milk both cows, sell the milk, sell one of the cows, and buy a bull.

———————

BUREAUCRACY: The government takes both cows, milks them, and pours the milk down the drain.

A man traveling by plane was in urgent need of using the men's room. Each time he tried the door it was occupied. The stewardess, aware of his predicament, suggested that he use the ladies' room, but cautioned him against pressing any of the buttons on the wall. The buttons were marked "WW," "WA," "PP," and "ATR." Eventually his curiosity got the better of him, and sitting on the potty, he carefully pressed the first button marked "WW." Immediately warm water sprayed gently over his entire ass. He thought, golly, the gals really have it made. Still curious he pressed the next button marked "WA." Warm air dried his ass completely. This, he thought, was out of this world. The button marked "PP" yielded a large powder puff which patted his bottom lightly with a scented powder. Naturally, he just couldn't resist the last one marked "ATR." When he awoke in the hospital, he panicked and buzzed for the nurse. When she appeared, he cried out, "What happened? The last thing I remember I was in the ladies' room aboard a plane."

The nurse replied, "Yes, you were, but you were cautioned about pressing the buttons. You were really having a great time until you pressed the button marked 'ATR,' which stands for Automatic Tampon Remover. Your penis is under your pillow."

A priest wanted to raise money for his church and being told that there was a fortune to be made in thoroughbred racing, he decided to purchase a horse and enter it in the races. However, at the auction, the going prices were so steep, he ended up buying a donkey instead.

He figured that since he had it, he might as well enter it in the races, and to his amazement the donkey came in third. The news headline read:

PRIEST'S ASS SHOWS

The priest was so pleased he entered it again. This time the donkey won. The following day, the papers read:

PRIEST'S ASS OUT IN FRONT

The Bishop was upset by this kind of publicity. So he ordered the priest never again to enter the donkey in another race. This time the headline read:

BISHOP SCRATCHES PRIEST'S ASS

This was just too much for the Bishop and he ordered the priest to get rid of the donkey. The priest decided to give it to a nun in a convent. The paper's headline read:

NUN HAS BEST ASS IN TOWN

The Bishop fainted and upon recovering, requested the nun to dispose of the donkey. She finally found a farmer who bought it for $10. The paper's headline now read:

NUN PEDDLES ASS FOR TEN DOLLARS

After this they buried the Bishop and the headlines read:

TOO MUCH ASS KILLS BISHOP

What's bad about being an atheist when you make love?

There's no one to talk to when you climax!

What's the ultimate rejection?

When you're masturbating and your hand falls asleep.

A really conceited guy is fucking this really conceited girl and she says, "Aren't I tight?"

He says, "No, just full."

What do you call a female clone?

A clunt.

Which of the following doesn't belong? Meat, eggs, wife, or a blowjob?

A blowjob, 'cause you can beat your wife, eggs or meat, but you can't beat a blowjob.

Did you hear about the guy who called his girlfriend "Tapioca" because she could be made in a minute?

Johnny Lyons says that one thing great about Joking Off is that you can joke off all you want, and you don't have to look your best!

Do you know why hunting season begins in November?

Because that's when the elections begin, and all the turkeys come out.

Two people were screwing in the middle of the road and a truck was headed right for them. The truck driver honked and honked, but the two people wouldn't move. Finally, he slammed on his brakes and stopped two feet away from them. The truck driver got out of the truck and yelled, "What's wrong with you? Didn't you see me coming?"

And the man replied yes and said, "I was coming, she was coming, you were coming, but you were the only one that had brakes."

Did you hear about the girl who was pregnant?

I told her not to play frisbee with her diaphragm!

STILL JOKING OFF

From birth to age eighteen, a girl needs good parents. From 18 to 35, she needs good looks. From 35 to 55 she needs a good personality, and from 55 on she needs cash.

Bill Clinton was at a political meeting recently and somebody asked him what he thought of the abortion bill. He asked, "Didn't I pay that?"

Recently, this old joke took on a new flavor:
Bill Clinton, Jesse Jackson, and Newt Gingrich were on an ocean liner. Suddenly the boat sprang a leak, and emergency lights began flashing all over. Reverend Jackson cried out, "Save the women and children!"
Newt Gingrich said, "Fuck the women and children!"
Bill Clinton said, "Do we have time?"

A young man was working in the royal stables when one morning the Crown Prince came in and yelled at him, "Attention! I want you to arrange your finest carriage—we've just received word that the Royal Princess is coming! Please decorate the carriage with flowers and plumes and make it look good!" As the young man was getting the carriage together, he noticed that one of the horses had an enormous erection and he said to the horse, "You'd think the Princess was coming to see you!"

A woman is in a psychiatrist's office and says to her doctor, "Please . . . kiss me!"
The doctor responds, "That's all I need. Isn't it enough that we're naked and I'm lying on top of you?"

A wealthy man with three girlfriends had a tough decision to make. He didn't know which one to choose, so he decided to give them each a thousand dollars, and observe how they spent it. So, he gave the blonde a thousand dollars, the brunette with big tits a thousand dollars, and the redhead a thousand dollars. A few days later he asked the blonde what she did with the money, and she said she went out and had her hair done, had a manicure, bought a few dresses, and perfume just so she could smell and look good for him. Then he asked the brunette what she did, and she claimed she took a three-day vacation in Puerto Rico so she could come home to him. Then he asked the redhead what she did. She said she invested the money wisely, made a $5,000 profit, wanted to give him back the thousand plus split the profit, and she gave him four thousand dollars.

Do you know which gal the man chose? The one with big tits, naturally!

A man walks into the doctor's office and describes his problem: "Either my wife has AIDS or Alzheimer's—I don't know which."

The doctor tells him, "Bring her deep into the woods and leave her there. If she comes home, don't fuck her."

Sex—for men—is just like banking. First you make a deposit, then you make a withdrawal. Then you lose interest!

Did you hear what Bill Clinton said to the new intern?

I don't think I've come across your face before.

STILL JOKING OFF 27

A guy walks into the doctor's office and says to the doctor, "Why is sex a pain in the ass to me?"

The doctor replies, "You're doing it wrong!"

A man walks into the pharmacy and asks the clerk for some sexlax. The pharmacist replies, "You mean Ex-lax."

The man says, "No, I mean sexlax—I don't have any trouble going!"

A woman goes to a gynecologist because she can't conceive and wants to be artificially inseminated. She disrobes in the doctor's office, lies down on the table and spreads her legs. The doctor, upon seeing this, takes off his pants and exposes his erect penis and immediately thrusts it into her. The woman says, "Oh my God, what's going on?"

The doctor replies, "I'm sorry Mrs. Jones, but I'm out of the bottle type. Please don't be upset—you have to settle for draft!"

A very extravagant brothel had a school for prostitutes in its basement. One day in class the teacher asked Maria, "How do you identify an elderly man in the dark?"

Maria responded, "It ain't hard."

An attractive young campaign supporter fancied a Presidential candidate in the 1996 elections. It was guaranteed that this politician would have her vote. At the end of the campaign, she finally got close enough to him to feel the sexual electricity she felt existed between them. No debate about it—these people wanted to get together. They went into the rear of the campaign headquarters, and the rather elderly politician, now embarking on climbing the highest mountain of his campaign trail, had a big problem. He knew how to solve it, but he couldn't dick at this moment—it was not what the doctor ordered. After a frustrating forty-five minutes the politician jumped to his feet and announced with disappointed ire, "Now I've failed to live up to my speech and bring matters to a climax. I hope you appreciate that I'm very sorry about this, and that you'll accept my apology. Now I want to state, for the record, that there was no wrongdoing. And, as always, I gave it everything that I had. As you know, it's been a long, tough campaign trail. However, after I'm elected, I promise you. . . ."

A young, recently married woman found herself on a television game show. Her entire family and all of her friends were viewing, and she was extremely nervous. The game show host asked the first question, "For five thousand dollars, who was the first woman?" She responded, "That's very easy: Eve."

The emcee exclaimed, "That's exactly right. Now for seventy-five thousand dollars, who was the first man?" The woman responded, "Adam." The host exclaimed, "You're absolutely right!"

"And now for ninety thousand dollars, what was the first thing Eve said to Adam in the Garden of Eden?" The woman answered, "Wow, that's a hard one." The host said, "You're exactly right!"

An elderly couple returns home from a night out on the town. The husband immediately starts to pack his bags. The wife asks, "Where are you going?"

He replies, "I'm going to Bali."

"Bali?" she asks, "Why Bali?"

The man says, "Simple. Every time you make love there they give you $10."

The woman then immediately starts packing her bags. And her husband asks, "Where are you going?"

"I'm going to Bali, too."

The husband questions why she is going. She replies, "I want to see how you are going to live on $20 a year!"

Two private detectives were doing some research on a scandalous divorce case in Los Angeles. At the husband's request they staked out the wife's bedroom, and, sure enough, she had another man inside. The detectives remarked to one another that they were going at it like sex was going out of style. After watching rather furtively for quite a few minutes, one detective finally said, "As long as we're here on the case, maybe we should go in after him?"

To this the other replied, "Great idea! Who first?"

A beautiful young woman goes to a psychiatrist. She thought she was a robot, because she had been made by a scientist!

It was very late, about 5 a.m. and Maria's father was still lying awake in the upstairs bedroom, waiting for Maria and her boyfriend to stop petting in the living room downstairs. Finally, in a fit of rage, the father jumped out of bed, ran to the top of the stairs and screamed, "Maria, is that guy fucking you?"

Maria replied, "No, but thanks for the idea!"

Joan and her new girlfriend Barbara were talking about a rather severe argument Joan had with her boyfriend, Johnny. "He kissed me so many times before we started fighting and once the fight began, he didn't kiss me for nearly two weeks, and then we made up," Joan told her.

Barbara replied, "But then I suppose he kissed you all over again?"

"No, only on my pussy!"

A man was shopping in the men's department at Bloomingdales, when he noticed an absolutely beautiful woman behind the sales counter. He went up to her and said, "Good morning, madam." She smiled pleasantly. "And what do you want?"

The man said, "I would like to wrap my arms around you and squeeze you tight, run my hands up and down your bottom, squeeze you, and then run my hands along your inner thighs and run them up underneath your dress and come to your sweet love hole and lightly finger it and then simultaneously unbutton your blouse with my teeth and suck on your beautiful tits and then bite your nipples lightly. . . . What I need is a new tie!"

A young boy to his mother: "Mother, how do lions fuck?"

"I don't know dear. Your father's a pig!"

A man comes home from work early and suddenly discovers that his wife is giving the paperboy a blowjob. He starts screaming and yelling at her, "How could you give the paperboy a blowjob when it's the milkman we owe?

Every neighborhood has its own Casanova, and George was the one who always got the most pussy on his block. When he smiled he had pussy written all over his face. Unfortunately, lately his prowess had fallen off a bit.

STILL JOKING OFF

George went to his doctor to complain about what was happening. The doctor was in awe; he couldn't believe it. "George," he said, "how could this happen? Everyone in the area knows you as the king of pussy—you have an incredible reputation."

George continued to complain to the doctor and said, "What good is a reputation if you can't make it stand up!"

You know you're getting older when . . . your friends tell you you haven't changed a bit.

You know you're getting older when . . . you're pretty certain there is nothing wrong with your eyes and the reason you can't see things is because the light is dim and the type is too small.

You know you're getting older when . . . you can no longer easily sleep until noon!

Do you know what the definition of a gynecologist is?

A spreader of wives tails!

A beautiful young Catholic girl went to confession, and the priest immediatley recognized her voice. After confession, he invited her to wait for him, and when he had heard all the other confessions, he invited her to come into the back of the church with him. Once there, he said that he wanted to review what she had confessed. He started by putting his arm around her, and he asked if the man had done that. She said, "Yes, Father."

He then kissed her, and asked her if the man had done

that. "Yes, Father, and much worse." The priest then lifted up her dress and started to play with her pussy, and asked if the man had done that.

"Yes, Father, and more!" The priest was very excited, and he pulled off the girl's panties and started to screw her.

Afterwards, he asked, "Did the young man do that to you, too?"

She answered: "Yes, Father, but it was worse, much worse!"

"But what could be worse than that?"

"Well, Father," said the girl, "I think he gave me herpes!"

Part Three

FOOD JOKES

Remember that the person who always appears to be buttering up to someone usually can't cut the mustard.

———

It's been said that politicians are not necessarily heroes to many people. They've all got lots of dough, but they're full of baloney!

———

What's in a honeymoon salad?

Lettuce alone!

———

When Marilyn was given her first matzoh ball, she said, "Mmm! Delicious! Can you eat any other part of the animal?

———

A guy, upon seeing a vampire, put a strand of garlic around his neck. Just his luck—the vampire's name is Guido.

A Jewish man goes into a Jewish delicatessen in New York, and is served by a Chinese waiter who is speaking fluent Hebrew. When the man is paying, he asks the owner of the deli, "Tell me, how come you've got a Chinese waiter that speaks Hebrew?"

He says, "Not so loud. He thinks he's speaking English!"

What is the condition when your toes get infected?

Toemain Poisoning!

Two priests came to meet a bishop. While waiting to see the bishop, one of the Church's servants served them some coffee and cakes. One of the cakes was a bit larger than the others. So the first priest said, "After you."

The other priest replied, "No, after you."

The first priest then said, "No, I insist, you take first choice!" This went on until finally one of the priests helped himself first to the big piece of cake. The other priest was visibly outraged. The one who had taken the cake said, "What?"

The angry priest replied, "You served yourself first, and you took the bigger cake!"

The first priest said, "So? If you had chosen first, which cake would you have taken?"

"Why, the smaller one, naturally?"

So the first priest said, "Well, then what are you complaining about? You got what you wanted, didn't you?"

STILL JOKING OFF

A man enters a new Jewish delicatessen and says to the waiter, "Waiter, what's with this chicken soup?"

"What do you mean, what's with this chicken soup?"

The man says, "It tastes funny."

The waiter says, "So . . . laugh?"

An Italian momma made pasta, and she got up early every morning, at five o'clock, to make pasta sauce for her family. One morning at five o'clock, she had made the pasta, and around ten o'clock she reached up into the cupboard to get some salt, and accidently knocked a whole box of BB's into the sauce. Since she had already spent all morning making the sauce, she figured it was too late to start over. So they had dinner that night and everyone ate the spaghetti sauce.

The next day her little girl told her, "Momma, Momma, I just took a crap and there were pellets in there."

So the momma said, "Don't worry, it's all right, it will pass."

A few minutes later her other daughter said, "Momma, I just took a crap and there were pellets in there."

So her momma said, "Don't worry, it will pass."

Finally, her son came downstairs and said, "Momma, you won't believe it."

And she said "I know, I know, you just took a crap and there were pellets in there."

And he answered, "No, I was whacking off and I shot the dog!"

What do you call the milk you get from the mammary glands?

Erogenized milk!

Gloria was telling Sam, "You won't believe this, but my husband goes into the bathtub with a fishing pole. Once into the tub, he throws a line into the toilet bowl."

"That's amazing," replies Sam. "Have you taken him in to see a psychiatrist?"

"No, I'm too busy cleaning the fish!"

You know you're getting older when ... not getting a little action means your prune juice is not working!

You know you're getting older when ... bran, fruit, and figs become a regular part of your diet!

You know you're getting older when ... you start to grow pleased with your shape and figure, finding it both attractive and aerodynamically sound.

What do you call nerds who work at the Quaker Oats factory?

Checkerboard squares!

I was recently driving through a part of Connecticut and I suddenly realized I was in a yuppie neighborhood. You know how I could tell? The fire department was putting out a fire using Perrier water!

Do you know what is the difference between a Southern delicacy and an ice cream used in a sexual act?

One is a corn pone and the other one is a porn cone!

STILL JOKING OFF

Do you know why cannibals become excited when women in a neighboring tribe become pregnant?

Because they know where the next meal is coming from!

Do you ever wake up in the morning and know you aren't going to have a good day?

It's when you wake up, look in the refrigerator and the rump roast farts in your face.

Can you name a food eaten by white racists?

Klan chowder!

What's the difference between a Scotsman and a coconut?

You can always get a drink from a coconut!

A grammar school teacher was teaching a class about the meaning of nutrition. She asked little Johnny what are the most important qualities of mothers' milk. Johnny replied, "It's fresh, nutritious, served at just the right temperature and it comes in beautiful containers!"

Did you hear about the new drink called a "pile driver?"

It's one part vodka and one part prune juice.

Do you know what they call frozen holy water in the Catholic Church?

Pope-sicles!

Janet and her girlfriend were out talking about sex and her girlfriend explained that her new boyfriend always wants to perform cunnilingus. Janet told her, "You don't know how lucky you are, but if you want to prevent him from doing that, why don't you rub some garlic on your pussy?"

Her girlfriend said, "Janet, I tried that, but the next night he came to bed with some bread and olive oil!"

Where do you find the most fish?

Between the head and the tail!

The owner of an Italian deli in New York lived over the store. One night he heard some funny noises coming from the shop. He went down there and found his beautiful sixteen-year-old daughter sitting on top of the counter, masturbating with a pepperoni. He was in awe, but didn't let out a peep and went back upstairs and went to bed. The next morning a customer came in and asked for some pepperoni. The owner said that he didn't have any. But the woman saw the pepperoni hanging there and became very upset. "What's that hanging over there?" she demanded.

"Well, madam, that's my son-in-law!"

A group of women got together on a regular basis, and they usually discussed families or local gossip. But they decided to change things a bit, and discuss important political issues, Bosnia, the Middle East, Afghanistan, etc. So one of the women said, "But what about Red China?"

To which another woman responded, "Fantastic—it looks especially good on a white tablecloth!"

Part Four

HOLLYWEIRD!

Ronald Reagan said that the way some children of celebrities write books critical of their parents helps you understand why certain species of this world eat their young!

Phyllis Diller said that for years she used wrinkle cream, and sure enough, she finally got wrinkles!

It's a jungle out there. You gotta look out for #1, but don't step in #2.

A lot of actors today claim they have watched television grow from infancy to adultery!

Did you hear about the new S&M series on television this fall?

It's called "GAG ME AND LACE ME!"

How many agents does it take to change a lightbulb?

Three! One to change the bulb, and two to try and kick the ladder out from under him!

A Jewish entertainment attorney is in Los Angeles. He's lounging around the pool of a fancy Bel Air mansion, and he hears an argument going on at the other end of the house. He leans over and asks a friend, "What's going on?"

The man replies, "It's a battle of wits."

So the attorney asks, "What, here in Hollywood? Who?"

The man answers, "Horowitz, Markowitz, and Leibowitz."

Groucho Marx was caught swimming in a WASP swimming pool in a fancy country club in Bel Air. The pool attendant came over and told him he'd have to stop swimming because he was Jewish.

Groucho then asked, "And what about my son? He's only half-Jewish. Can he go in up to his waist?"

A Hollywood entertainment attorney is talking with his client, Mr. Albert. Mr. Albert says, "I'd be happy to hire you, if you're absolutely positive you could win the case."

The lawyer says, "Please tell me what the story is."

Mr. Albert then begins to tell the story of some very complicated fraud and cheating going on in the movie business. Then the lawyer says, "It appears to be an open and shut case."

Mr. Albert says, "Oh my God, that's horrible!"

"Why so?"

"I just told you my business partner's side of the story!"

Never marry an actress ... or any other kind of female impersonator.

—Mort Sahl

Three people die and go to heaven. St. Peter interviews them at the pearly gates and asks the first man, "Well, how much did you earn in 1998?"

The first man replies, "About two million dollars!" St. Peter directs him to the gate marked "Executives."

The next man comes up and St. Peter asks, "How much did you earn?"

The man replies, "I'm an attorney in New York and I earned $200,000." St. Peter directs him to the gate labeled "Professionals."

The third man comes up and St. Peter asks him about his income and the man replies, "Well, I earned $3,500."

St. Peter said, "Okay, you go over to the door labeled 'Actors.'"

A new TV game show in Hollywood had many contestants who were beautiful, but they weren't necessarily too smart. On one show, one such woman was extremely nervous, but tried to make the best of her performance. The host asked her: "Who was the first man, for one thousand dollars?"

She responded, "The first man was Peter, my postman ... but he only paid me $100!"

A while back, there was a famous columnist in Hollywood by the name of Hedda Hopper. Many famous actors sought her out—it was rumored she gave good Hedda!

A very famous actress was under a major contract to one of the biggest studios in Hollywood. She was troubled by a vaginal disorder, and was sent to the studio doctor before re-signing what was going to be the biggest contract in the history of Hollywood. The doctor examined the woman and was in total awe. He said, "Oh my God, what a big pussy you have! Oh my God, what a big pussy you have!"

"I know," replied the actress. "but why did you have to say it twice?"

The doctor said, "I didn't!"

A beggar knocked on the door of a Beverly Hills mansion. There was no immediate answer, so the bum kept knocking. For fifteen minutes he kept this up. Finally, an angry millionaire opened the door. The beggar said, "Can I have two dollars?"

"What the hell are you doing waking me up at 3 o'clock in the morning just for two dollars?" demanded the millionaire. The bum replied, "I don't tell you how to run your business, so don't you tell me how to run mine."

What Hollywood personality developed faster than a Polaroid snapshot?

Dolly Parton.

Do you know what Bill Clinton's pet name for Monica Lewinsky is?

My little humidor.

STILL JOKING OFF

Do you know what the difference between a youthful starlet and a prostitute is?

A prostitute doesn't drive a Ferrari!

Why didn't Dolly Parton pursue a career in theater?

She was afraid of being a big bust on Broadway!

Do you know what Dolly Parton's favorite candybar is?

Mounds!

What do you get when you cross Arnold Schwarzenegger with a Jewish man from the garment district in New York?

Conan the Wholesaler!

An attractive young actress had been suffering headaches, which she felt were stress-related, so she made an appointment with the psychiatrist reported to be the best in Beverly Hills. Immediately after entering his office, the doctor said to the woman, "Please take your clothes off, and lie down on the couch."

The actress did, and the doctor lay down on top of her, and proceeded to screw her.

After he was done, he said: "OK, that takes care of my problems. Now let's hear about yours!"

Part Five

ETHNIC JOKES

Black Jokes

A white baby dies and goes to heaven and gets a pair of wings. What do you call him?

An angel.

A black baby dies and goes to heaven and gets a pair of wings. What do you call him?

A bat!

Why did God give blacks rhythm?

Because he fucked up their hair.

Why do blacks wear turtlenecks?

To hide their flea collars.

Why do black people smell so bad?

So the blind can hate them too.

Did you hear about the new war movie they're making with an all-black cast?

It's called "Apackoflips Now".

How many blacks does it take to pave a driveway?

It depends on how thin you slice them.

Did you hear about Ku Klux Knievel?

He tried to jump over eight blacks with a steam roller.

What do you call four blacks in a Cadillac?

Grand auto theft.

Did you ever see Ray Charles's wife?

Neither has he.

Why don't they have any black snow skiers?

Because their lips explode at 1000 feet.

What's black and white and has three eyes?

Sammy Davis, Jr. and his wife.

STILL JOKING OFF 55

Why did they build the Bay Bridge?

So blacks could swim over in the shade.

What color is a black when you run over him?

Flat black.

What do you get when you cross a black and a gorilla?

A dumb gorilla.

Why don't blacks drive convertibles?

Because their lips would flap them to death.

Why do black people want to move to Taiwan?

So they can be called tycoons.

A black walked into a bar with a beautiful parrot on his shoulder. The bartender asked, "Where did you get that?"
The parrot said, "Africa."

A black guy was washing windows on the outside of the sixteenth floor of the Empire State building. An angel came along and said, "Why don't you step back and admire your work?"
The black guy answered, "I can't do that—I'll fall."
The angel said, "Listen, I'm an angel, I wouldn't tell you to step back if you were going to fall. Look at me, I'm

not falling." So the black guy figured an angel wouldn't lead him astray and he stepped back and plummeted to the ground. The angel said to himself, "I can't believe they let me be an angel the way I hate blacks."

A black panther in the forest walks up to a pond and sees his reflection. And he says to himself, "I am so beautiful. Look at me. Look at my beautiful black coat and my beautiful rippling muscles and my beautiful green eyes. I is the most beautiful animal in the kingdom." The panther walks along and comes across a toad. And he says, "Look at you, man. You is so ugly. You got that crinkly skin and them blotches all over the place and you all scrunched up and shit."

And the toad says, "Fuck you, man. I've been sick!"

What do you call one white guy with one black guy?

Liberal.

What do you call one white guy with three black guys?

A victim!

What do you call one white guy with five black guys?

Church!

What do you call one white guy with ten black guys?

A quarterback!

STILL JOKING OFF

What do you call one white guy with fifty black guys?

Boss!

What do you call a white guy with a thousand black guys?

Warden!

What do you call a white guy with twenty thousand black guys?

Postmaster General!

What do you call a white guy with two million black guys?

Prime Minister of Rhodesia!

Two young black men from Georgia were driving around looking for women and couldn't find any. They found a pig along the road and pulled over, jumped out and put it on the seat between them. As they continued to drive around, they suddenly heard the sound of a police siren. The driver looked in the mirror, saw flashing lights right behind him and pulled over. Immediately they decided they didn't want to get caught with a stolen pig, so they put a sheet over it. The cop pulled over, walked up to the car and asked, "What are you two doing driving around here?"

One replied, "Well, Officer, we were just looking for women." Suddenly there was a little noise and the pig's head popped up.

The officer was in awe and shook his head, "Could you tell me what a nice young filly like you is doing with these two Negroes?"

Polish Jokes

Did you hear about the Polack who . . .

Looked in his lumberyard for a Draft Board!

Did you hear about the Polish gambler who . . .

Took a roll of toilet paper to a crap game!

How about the Polack who . . .

Lost his girlfriend because he couldn't remember where he laid her!

Then there was the Polack who . . .

Wore a union suit because his wife was having labor pains!

What about the Polack who . . .

Thought "no kidding" meant birth control!

How could we forget the Polack who . . .

Thought Peter Pan was something to put under the bed!

Did you hear about the Polack who . . .

Smelled good only on the right side? He didn't know where to buy Left Guard!

What about the Polack who . . .

Bought his wife a washer and dryer for Christmas? A douche bag and towel!

Then there was the Polack who . . .

Thought a mushroom was a place to neck!

What about the Polack who . . .

Went to the outhouse, put one leg in each hole, and shit in his pants!

A POLISH MOTHER WRITING TO HER SON

Dear Son:

Just a few lines to let you know that I'm still alive. I'm writing this letter slowly because I know that you cannot read fast. You won't know the house when you come home—we've moved.

About your father—he has a lovely new job. He has 500 men under him. He is cutting the grass at the cemetery.

There was a washing machine in the new house when we moved in, but it isn't working too good. Last week I put fourteen shirts into it, pulled the chain, and I haven't seen the shirts since.

Your sister, Mary, had a baby this morning. I haven't found out whether it is a boy or a girl, so I don't know whether you're an aunt or uncle.

Your Uncle Dick drowned last week in a vat of whiskey in Dublin Brewery. Some of his workmates dived in to save him, but he fought them off bravely. We cremated his body, and it took three days to put out the fire.

Your cousin, Stash, has a good job doing construction work. Up until then he thought manual labor was a Mexican.

Your father didn't have much to drink at Christmas. I put a bottle of castor oil in his pint of beer. It kept him going 'til New Year's Day. By the way, he received the shirt you sent him with his initials on the sleeve. He said it was the first monogramed handkerchief he ever owned.

It only rained twice last week. First for three days, and then for four days. Monday it was so windy that one of our chickens laid the same egg four times.

We had a letter yesterday from the undertaker. He said if the last installment wasn't paid on your grandmother within seven days, up she comes.

Your loving mother

P.S. I was going to send you $10.00 but I had already sealed the envelope.

P.P.S. If you don't receive this letter, let me know right away.

Why don't Polish woman breast-feed their babies?

Because it hurts to boil their nipples!

Why don't Polish people eat pickles?

Because they can't fit their heads in the jar!

Did you hear about the Polish parachute?

It opens on impact!

How do you tell how many Polacks live in a town?

Count the cellar windows and multiply by 36.

Why don't they let Polacks swim in Lake Michigan?

Because they leave a ring!

STILL JOKING OFF

Why do Polacks carry shit in their wallets?

For identification!

A Polack and a black jump out of a plane at the same time, who hits first?

Who cares?!

What do you call a Polack with an I.Q. of 176?

A village!

Did you hear about the Polack who studied five days for a urine test?

Did you hear about the Polack who thought asphalt was a rectal problem?

What happens if a Polack doesn't pay his garbage bill?

They stop delivering.

Did you hear about the Polack who tried to throw himself on the ground and missed?

Why do Polacks put shit next to bridesmaids during a wedding?

To keep the flies off the bride!

What is the Polish idea of matched luggage?

Three shopping bags from the same super market.

How can you tell the Polack at a cock fight?

He's the one holding the duck!

Why did the Polish grandmother have her Fallopian tubes tied?

She didn't want to have any more grandchildren!

Did you hear about the Polish father who locked the keys in his car?

It took him two hours to get his family out.

A Polish man was reading the classified ads of the local newspaper, and read an ad calling for a "Male patient for special research project, $1,000.00. Stop by for details." The man decided to follow-up on the ad, and went to the address the following morning. When he got there he was greeted by a man in a white lab coat, and taken into a conference room where he met several doctors. One of the doctors explained that this is a special experiment attempting to determine if male humans can mate with female gorillas, and that he would have to have sex with a gorilla. They then ask him if he is still interested. The man thought for a minute, and agreed to do it, but with three conditions: "I won't French kiss the gorilla. Second, I won't let anyone watch. And third, I can't possibly pay the $1,000.00 in one payment; can I pay it off monthly?"

STILL JOKING OFF

Do you know why the Polish man took his necktie back to the haberdashery?

It was too tight!

Did you hear about the Polish man that went ice fishing?

He came home with a bag full of ice!

Hispanic Jokes

What do you say to a Puerto Rican in a three-piece suit?

"Will the defendant please rise!"

If Tarzan was Puerto Rican, what would Cheetah be?

Puerto Rican!

Why don't Puerto Ricans have checking accounts?

Because it's hard to sign a check with a spray can!

Why do Mexicans have refried beans?

Have you ever heard of a Mexican doing anything right the first time?

How come the Mexican army only used 600 Mexicans at the Alamo?

Because they only had two cars!

How does God make Puerto Ricans?

He sandblasts blacks!

How do you keep Mexicans out of your back yard?

Put your trash cans in your front yard!

Did you hear about the guy who thought Manual Labor was the President of Mexico?

Los Federales were looking for Pancho Villa when they came across a little man riding a burro. They stopped him and asked him if he'd seen Pancho Villa. He replied, "Who is Pancho Villa?"

"You know—the big man who wears a white uniform, rides a white horse and carries a big gun."

The man replied, "Oh sure, I saw him two days ago."

The federales asked, "What do you mean? What happened?"

The man said, "Well, I was riding alone, minding my own business, when Pancho Villa rode up to me, stopped me and made me get off my burro. At that time, my burro was taking a shit and Pancho Villa was very mean to me; he pointed his gun at me and told me to eat the burro shit. So what was I gonna do? He was pointing a gun at me, so I ate the burro shit. Then, when I finished he told me to eat more burro shit. But the burro, he no shit no more, so I hit the burro on the backside and he jumped and that made Pancho Villa's horse jump, which threw Pancho Villa off his horse and then his horse took a shit. So when Pancho Villa fell off, he dropped his gun and I picked it up and I pointed it at him and I told him to eat the horse shit. And he ate the horse shit. So you ask me if I've seen Pancho Villa? I had lunch with him two days ago!"

Two young male tourists were visiting Tijuana for the weekend. As they were walking along the street, a prostitute popped out of a doorway and cried, "Hey, guys, come on in. I'll give you something you've never had before."

Another guy on the street tapped one of the tourists on the shoulder and said, "You better get the hell out of here—she has leprosy."

Two men were in a Texas bar discussing the woman in the next town.

One told the other, "She has the biggest posse in El Puso!"

What do you call a man that's half Mexican and half black?

A wetblack!

Jewish Jokes

At a funeral for a very wealthy Jew, one of the mourners was pounding his chest and screaming and crying. The rabbi approaches him and says, "You poor man, you must have been a relative of the deceased?"

"No! No!" sobbed the man. "That's why I'm crying!"

How do you say "Fuck you" in Jewish?

Trust me!

Define Jewish foreplay.

Two hours of begging!

What do you get when you cross a Jew and a gypsy?

A chain of empty stores!

What happens to a Jewish man when he walks into a wall with a full erection?

He breaks his nose.

How do you cure a Jewish woman of nymphomania?

Marry her.

A recent survey showed that crime in the Jewish race was declining. A Jewish man, when asked why, said, "Easy, crime doesn't pay!"

A Jewish mother gave her son two neckties for his birthday, a paisley and a solid. The next day the son wore the solid tie, and the mother said, "So what's the matter with the paisley tie?"

What's the difference between a prostitute, a mistress and a Jewish American Princess? A prostitute says, "Your time is up!" A mistress says, "I need more time." And a JAP says, "Beige. I think I'll paint the ceiling beige."

An old Jewish woman was in a train berth near an intelligent younger man. After five minutes or so the woman shook her head and moaned, "Oh my God, am I thirsty!" About five minutes later the same thing, "Oh my God, am I thirsty!" After this had gone on for about half an hour, the man, who was bewildered by this woman's constant moaning, got up, ran down the corridor of the train, and returned to the berth with a cup of water.

He said to the woman, "Dear lady, drink this." He

STILL JOKING OFF

handed her the cup, then settled back into his seat and resumed his paperwork.

Five minutes later, the woman moaned again, "Oh my God, was I thirsty!"

Irving makes a decision to stop by and make a surprise visit to his friend Saul. When he arrives Saul is very carefully scraping the paint from the walls and placing it neatly into a cardboard box. Irving asked, "What are you doing? Are you repainting the house?

Saul replied, "No, we're moving!"

Four friends are on a train to Europe. One is French, another English, another Irish, and the fourth, a Jewish gentleman from Israel. They agree that in the event the train crashes, each survivor would put $1,000 in the deceased's graves to expedite getting them to heaven. Unfortunately, the train crashes and the Frenchman dies. The other three gentlemen go to his funeral and as agreed, the Irishman puts $1,000 into the grave, and the Englishman does the same. The Jew writes a check for $3,000 payable to the dead Frenchman and puts it into the grave and takes $2,000 change!

A panhandler who was working Wall Street one day approached a dignified business man and asked him for some money. The man replied, "I'm very sorry, but I never give money to people in the street."

The panhandler replied, "What should I do? Come up to your office?"

Father O'Connell was teaching catechism and came upon three small boys playing; one was a member of the class and two were strangers. Father was introduced to the strangers and told them he would give them five dollars if they could tell him who's the greatest man on earth. The boys think for a minute and one of the boys said, "The Pope."

The priest said, "Sure, he's a good man, but he certainly isn't the greatest." He then turned to the little boy in his class and asked him if he remembered. The boy replied, "St. Patrick, because he brought Christianity to Ireland." Father told him it was a good answer but not quite right.

Last, one of the strangers, a Jewish boy, said, "I know, sir. It was Jesus Christ!"

The priest smiled in a rather confused way and paid the Jew five dollars, telling him, "I'm certain that someone of your faith doesn't truly believe that."

The Jew replied, "Oh no, Father. I know Moses was the greatest but I wanted to win the money!"

Finkelstein asked Goldberg how his son the lawyer was doing. Goldberg replied, "He's doing fabulous—every young lawyer should do as well as he does. He's so busy at the firm that he can't take on any new cases and they've given him a raise. Very soon they are going to make him a partner." Finkelstein then asked about his daughter, Elizabeth, to which Goldberg replied, "She's a fabulous daughter. She just returned from Israel and won a full scholarship to Columbia Medical School."

"Well," Finkelstein asked, "How's your son Joseph?"

Goldberg replied, "Ah, he's still selling schmatas (clothing) in the Bowery. Without him, we'd be starving!"

There was an old Jewish woman who heard a song called "Two Lips and Seven Kisses." She called up information after hearing the song on the radio to get the name of the record company. In dialing she erroneously called up a gas station, and she asks, "Do you have 'Two Lips and Seven Kisses?' "

The gas station attendant who answered the phone said, "No, but I have two nuts and seven inches."

So the woman asked, "Is this a record?"

To which the man replied, "No, it's an average!"

How does a JAP make Manischewitz wine?

She squeezes his balls!

Why did God create Gentiles?

Without them, who would buy retail?

Do you know what you call a Japanese Jew?

Oryentl!

Do you know what sucks, but doesn't swallow?

A JAP!

What was the name of the first Jewish astronaut?

Nose Cohen!

Two old Jewish men are talking, and one said to the other, "Sylvia, my wife, is an angel."

The second man replied, "You're lucky—my wife is still alive!"

Italian Jokes

Do you know what Italians call an enema?

An innuendo!

Why don't Italians have freckles?

Because they slide off!

Did you hear about the Italian who was asked to be a Jehovah's Witness?

He refused to because he didn't see the accident!

How do you brainwash an Italian?

Give him an enema!

Why don't Italians eat fleas?

Because they can't get their little legs apart!

Why did God make urine yellow and come white?

So Italians could tell if they were coming or going!

What's the definition of a happy Roman?

Gladiator!

An old Italian man went to his doctor. "Doctor, please examine me. I need to see if I'm sexually fit."

The doctor said to him, "Okay, let me see your sex organs."

The man replied, "Oh my God!" and he stuck out his middle finger and his tongue.

Guido and Maria just got married, returned from their honeymoon, and moved into their apartment above Maria's parents in Little Italy. Early one morning Maria's parents heard the rhythmic beating of a bed bouncing up and down on the floor. The wife said, "Come on, let's do it!" And Maria's father rolled on top of her and screwed her brains out. When he was trying to go back to sleep, there was a repeat of the same sounds and his wife said again. "Come on, they can do it again, why can't we?" They screwed again and just as they were getting back to sleep they heard the bed springs squeaking again and the wife said, "Let's do it!"

At this, the father stood up on top of the bed and banged on the ceiling, screaming, "Guido and Maria, cut it out! What are you trying to do, kill us?!"

Gay Jokes

Why is San Francisco like granola?

Because once you get past the fruits and nuts all you have are the flakes!

Did you hear about the queer nail?

Laid in the road and blew a tire!

Did you hear about the queer Irishman?

He preferred women over whiskey!

What's the definition of a Gay Frenchman?

Gallis!

What's the difference between an oral and a rectal thermometer?

The taste!

Three faggots were sitting in a hot tub when a blob of come rose to the surface. So one of them said, "All right, who farted?"

Two gay men are standing around watching a dog lick his balls.
One man say "Gee, I wish I could do that."
The other man says, "Don't you think you should get to know him first?"

A gay man walks into a bar, walks up to one of the patrons sitting at the bar, and says, "Excuse me, sir. Do you mind if I push your stool in a little?"

A gay guy walks into a butcher shop and says, "Give me some pepperoni," to the butcher.
The butcher says, "Would you like that sliced?"
The gay guy replies, "What do you think I am going to do, put it in a piggy bank?"

A nun gets into a cab in New York City and tells the driver that she would like to go to Brooklyn. The nun says to the driver, "I've been a nun for twenty years and I've always been a virgin, but I've always wanted to have sex with a man. However, I would have to have sex under these conditions: First, that the man is not married; second, that he be single and third, that since I am a virgin he would have to perform anal sex with me."

The cabbie says to the sister, "I just happen to fit your criteria: I'm single, I'm not married, and I would be happy to have anal intercourse with you." So they pull over and do the dirty deed and the cabbie rides the Hershey highway. They continue with the drive and the cab driver says to the sister, "I'm sorry. I lied. I'm really a married man."

The nun says to the cab driver, "I have to be honest with you too. I lied. My name is Frank and I'm on my way to a costume party."

Two young men were walking in the park talking about their sex lives. Peter says, "You know, you are what you eat, and that's why you're a cunt."

His friend says, "You're right. We are what we eat and that's why you're a prick."

A few gay men were having a discussion and one said to the others, "I don't want you to think I'm prejudiced, but you can always tell a Jewish faggot." The other gays replied that it must be the way their peckers are shaped. But the first one replied, "No, it's the words they use when they speak in private about someone's private parts, so to speak." They then asked: "What does a Jew faggot say?"

"He blew."

A homosexual goes to a gay doctor and says, "Doctor, if I were bitten by a rattlesnake, what would you do?" The doctor told him he would suck out the poison. The patient then asks, "What would you do if a rattlesnake bit me on the cock?"

The doctor replied, "Don't worry. You'd live forever!"

Do you know what a queer Arab is?

He's the one who speaks with tongue in sheik!

Do you know what they call a drag race in San Francisco?

Of course, they call it rush hour!

Do you know what they call a bicycle rider who is bisexual?

Bi-cyclist!

Do you know what the definition of latent homosexuality is?

Wishful thinking.

Do you know what the Moral Majority and faggots have in common?

They both suck!

What is the difference between a vulture and a faggot?

A vulture won't eat a man until he's dead!

What do you call a prick with V.D., AIDS, and gonorrhea?

A hot dog with the works!

STILL JOKING OFF

Do you know what they call a gay bar that doesn't have any stools?

A fruit stand!

What's worse than an angry black man with a knife?

A faggot with a chipped tooth!

What do they call a faggot who teaches other faggots how to give blowjobs?

A head master.

Two couples went on a vacation in the Poconos, into the mountains, bringing tents, campfire materials and traps. As the first adventurous day went on, it became bedtime. One of them suggested that they switch bed partners, which everyone agreed to. Later that night, one man turned to his bed partner and said, "I'm having a tremendous amount of fun. Do you think the girls are having as much fun as we are?"

There was an old man from Nantucket
whose dick was so long
he could suck it.
He said, with a grin,
as he wiped off his chin,
"If my ears were a cunt,
I would fuck it."

A gay man usually gets a cup of coffee in the neighborhood café every afternoon. When the kids came in after school they greeted him with "Hello, cunt," to which he never reacted. But one day after the kids came in he screamed, "Don't call me that."

All the kids yelled, "Why not?"

The faggot said, "Because the other day I saw one."

Can you believe it? They're now making lesbian sneakers. Originally they were called "Dykies." But they had to recall them all, because the tongues weren't long enough!

Do you know why the gay athlete wouldn't drink anything after a race?

He was afraid he might contract Gatoraids!

What is a faggot's greatest fantasy?

Being stuck between a Rock and a hard place!

Two gay men had just met and were about to have sex together. One of them took off his pants, revealing an extremely large penis. The other man immediately left the room, and came back with a crayon. So the first man asked, "What are you doing?"

To which the second man responded, "With the crayon? Well, I have to draw the line somewhere!"

Three men were in the men's room at a bar, pissing in urinals next to one another. They got to talking, and the first man asked the second, "So, what's your name?"

The second man answered, "My name's McCoy."

At this the first man seemed startled, and said, "What a coincidence—my name's McCoy, too."

Then the third man said, "This is unbelievable—my name's McCoy, too."

So then the first man asked the second, "What do you do?" The second man said, "I work for a wine company, I'm a cork soaker. What do you do?"

And the first man said, "I work for a soft-drink company. I'm a coke-sacker."

So they both turned to the third man, who smiled and said, "I'm the real McCoy!"

A very faithful homosexual couple, Pietro and Alberto, are spending an evening at home. Alberto says, "Hey, Pietro, did the paperboy come yet?"

Pietro answers, "No, but he's got a very funny look in his eyes!"

Miscellaneous Ethnic Jokes

How many Californians does it take to screw in a lightbulb?

None. Californians screw in hot tubs!

———

How many lawyers does it take to change a lightbulb?

Five! One to change the bulb, and four to do the screwing!

———

How many psychiatrists does it take to change a lightbulb?

One, but the lightbulb has to be willing to change!

———

People who can fix the blame are a dime a dozen, but the ones who get ahead are the ones who can fix the trouble!

———

Most children are like politicians. You only see them when they need help!

Some people say that discussion is the exchange of knowledge, but argument is the exchange of ignorance!

One surefire fact is that you can always get the truth from an American politician after he has turned 70, or given up all hope of becoming president.

One of the big problems with politics in Washington today is the "wind chill factor." The Senate and the Congress provide the wind and the public gets the chills!

A blind man and his seeing-eye dog were walking down the street. As they proceeded, the dog guided the man around garbage cans, open stairwells and even a crack in the sidewalk. When they reached the corner, the traffic light was red and the dog stopped. The dog lifted his leg and peed on the blind man, who in turn, offered him a bone. Two people observing this asked the blind man why, when the dog obviously saved him from injury earlier, he did nothing, but now, after the dog wet him, he rewarded the dog with a bone. The blind man said, "It's no reward. I'm trying to find out where his head is so I can kick him in the butt."

The cannibal chief came out of the woods and saw some of his people laughing and joking and dancing around a huge kettle over the fire. "Hey, what's happening?" asked the chief.

"Chiefie, we found this little guy wandering around. I brought him in."

The chief looked into the pot and asked, "Was he about 5 foot 4?"

"Yes."

"Did he have a fringe of hair around his bald head?"

"Yeah, Chief."

"Was he wearing a plain brown robe with a white rope around him?"

"Yeah, Chief."

"You fools. You shouldn't be boiling him. He's a friar."

A father says to his wife, "We're going to find out what Johnny wants to be when he grows up. Watch this." He puts a $10 bill on the table and says, "This represents a banker." Next to it he places a brand new bible. This, he says "represents a clergyman." Beside the bible he places a bottle of whisky, "and this," he says "represents a bum." The two of them hide where they can see the articles on the table. Pretty soon the kid comes into the room and spies the objects on the table. He looks around to see if he's alone. He doesn't see anyone, so he picks up the ten-spot, holds it up to the light, and puts it down. Then he fingers through the bible as he walks around. Then he quickly uncaps the bottle, smells the contents, and in one quick motion, he picks up the bill, stuffs it in his pocket, puts the bible under his arm, grabs the bottle, and walks out of the room whistling. The father then turns to his wife and says, "How about that! My God, he's going to be a politician."

Two men were seated at a bar on top of the Empire State Building. One man turned to the other and asked, "Do you know anything about this building?"

"No," replied the other man, "I'm from out of town."

"Well," the first man stated, "it's a fact that the wind is so strong at this height, that if someone were to jump off the top they'd never reach the ground. The wind would blow them right back up again."

"I may be from out of town," the second man said, "but I'm not a fool."

"Well, I'll prove it to you," the first man said. Before the second man could stop him, he flung himself over the edge. The second man watched in horror as the first hurtled toward the earth. And then, amazingly, the first man started to rise and landed back in his seat back at the bar.

"I don't believe it!" the second man exclaimed. "I've got to try that." But when he jumped, he did not stop falling and he hit the ground, smashing into a million bits.

The bartender turned to the first man and said, "Superman, you're a mean drunk."

A couple had their three children over to help them celebrate their fiftieth wedding anniversary. One was a successful lawyer, one a big-time doctor, and the daughter, a famous actress. "We did not have a chance to get you and Mom a present," said the two sons.

"I was doing a TV commercial and did not have time to get a present either," said the daughter.

After dinner, while having drinks in the living room the father called all three of them together and said, "You know something? Me and your mother never were married."

"Does this mean that we're . . . we're . . . well, you know what I mean," said the daughter.

The father said, "You're right. And three of the cheapest ones I've ever seen."

The old man lay dying. He turned to his wife, patted her hand, and said, "When I came home from the first war in 1918, Esther, you were by my side. And when I was freed from the concentration camp after the second war, you were by my side, too." Wiping a tear with his sleeve

STILL JOKING OFF

he continued, "When our little shop went bankrupt and we were left without a cent, you, Esther, were by my side. And now, now I am dying, and you are still by my side. Esther," he said, gazing hard at her, "you're a jinx."

A local fire department has just bought a brand-new Mercedes hook and ladder fire engine, and they decide to ask the local clergy to bless their new machine. A priest comes and splashes the truck with holy water, and says a few words in Latin. The pastor makes the sign of the cross, and prays: "May God help this equipment combat the evils of fire." A rabbi approaches the truck, wanders over to the engine, and cuts two inches off the hose!

Johnny Lyons would like to give you a little test on word twisting and that is, "What is the difference between a pickpocket and a Peeping Tom?"

A pickpocket snatches watches!

Do you know why Bill Clinton can't take a lie detector test?

You have to be able to establish a base line.

A Scotsman and his architect were surveying the land where he was having an enormous house constructed. As he was walking, he said to the architect, "Please don't remove that tree over there because directly under that tree is where I got laid for the first time."

The architect said, "Sir, that's so sentimental. Directly under that tree there, eh?"

"Yes," the Scotsman replied, "and you see that tree over there? Please don't disturb that either because that's where her mother stood while I was having sex for the first time."

The architect asked, "Her mother stood there when you were fucking her daughter?"

The Scotsman said "Of course!"

The architect asked, "What did her mother say?"

"Baahh!"

Three men arrive in heaven: an Italian, a Greek and a Jew. They plead with God to let them have one more chance on earth. He complies with the request but tells them they must give up the one thing they love most, or else they will return immediately to heaven. So they are put on the streets and almost immediately the Italian sees a pizza shop and goes in. He bites into the slice and disappears. The Greek and Jew continue to walk down the street. The Jew sees a dollar bill on the sidewalk and bends over to pick it up. The Greek disappears.

A man went to a psychiatrist, and said, "Doctor, I'm worried. I just bought a beautiful Great Dane for my son, and I think I'm in love with him."

The doctor asked, "You think you're in love with your son?"

And the man answered, "No, the dog!"

So the doctor said, "Affection for a pet isn't really that unusual."

Then the man said, "But I'm crazy about this dog, I want to love it. I try to hold it and caress it. I want to take it away with me on business trips, and weekends."

So the psychiatrist asked, "Could you tell me if the dog is a male or a female?"

At this the man became angry. "It's a female! What do you think—I'm some kind of pervert?!"

A lady buys a parrot, takes him home and the parrot says, "Let me squeeze your tits."

STILL JOKING OFF

She says, "Don't say that! Say 'Polly wants a cracker?'"
The parrot says, "Lemme squeeze your tits."
The lady says, "If you don't stop saying that I'm gonna put you in the freezer." He says it again and she puts him in the freezer. After a hour she opens the freezer and says, "I hope you've learned a lesson."
The parrot says, "Come on, lemme squeeze your tits!" The woman slams the freezer in disgust. Two hours later she opens up the freezer door and the parrot is really very, very cold.
She says, "I hope you have learned your lesson now."
The parrots says, "Lemme squeeze those titties!" The woman screams and slams the freezer door again and the parrot turns around and sees a 20 lb. frozen turkey and asks, "What did you do? Ask to lick her pussy?"

A group of guys were touring an Indian reservation in North Dakota and approached an Indian girl prostitute who was apparently looking for work. One of the men went up to her and said, "I'm interested in you. How much do you charge?"
She replied, "$500."
He responds, "That's too much money. The Indians sold Manhattan for only $24!"
The girl said, "That's quite possible," and she shook her hips a little bit and said, "but Manhattan just lies there!"

Do you know what you call a skinny WASP?

A Wisp!

Why were rectal thermometers banned in Libya?

There were too many reports of brain damage!

Do you know the difference between a Libyan and a box of shit?

A box.

A group of four men often got together to play racquetball. After the game, three of the men showered in the locker room, and then went and had a few drinks in the club bar. After this had been going on for some time, one of the three men asked the man who always left, "How come you never hang around and get cleaned up and have a few with us?" The fourth man seemed a little embarrassed, but he admitted that he didn't want to be seen in the shower with the other men because he felt his penis was small.

So the first man asked, "Does it work?"

"Of course, it works extremely well."

So the first man asked, "Would you like to trade it in for one that looks great in the shower?"

One winter day a man decided to go ice fishing, so he packed up his truck, drove out to the lake, cut a hole in the ice, and went to work. He had been at it for several hours without any luck when a young boy came along. This boy set up about twenty or thirty yards from the man, cut a hole in the ice, threw his line in, and immediately came up with a fish! Almost as soon as he had that one off the hook and dropped his line again, he pulled in another one. The man was perplexed, and two minutes later the kid pulled up another one. All this time the man still had no luck, so he finally walked over to the boy and asked, "Son, I've been here two or three hours and haven't caught a thing. You've been here ten minutes and you've got three fish. Tell me, what's your secret?" The kid looked up, and mumbled something incoherent. So the man

STILL JOKING OFF

asked again, "Come on, kid, what's your secret? I won't pass it around." And the kid, again, mumbled something the man can't understand. So the man, who was getting a little annoyed, said, "Look, kid, I just want to catch one stinking fish so the whole trip won't be a bust. What's your goddamn secret?"

So the kid looks up again, spits into his hand, and says, "You have to keep the worms warm!"

What do Arabian men do on weekend nights?

They lounge under palm trees and eat their dates!

What do you get when you cross Fidel Castro with a potato?

A dick-tater!

A young Arab man joined the army, and went off into the desert with his troops. One of the veterans was showing him the camp, and when they came to where the camels were housed, the veteran said to the recruit, "And since we have no women here in the desert, if it ever gets so bad, come here to get relief." The recruit was a little confused, but he didn't ask any questions. After a few weeks, it turned out he started to feel a little lonely, so he went to where the camels were kept, picked a likely camel, and started to kiss it. After a few minutes, he got used to it, and he was preparing to make love to the camel when that same veteran came in. He asked, "What are you doing?"

Suddenly, the recruit understood the system, and he said, "When you say relief, you mean we should take the camels and ride to where there are women?"

And the veteran soldier answered, "No, that's not the problem. It's just that this camel is a male!"

Part Six

VERY SICK JOKES

Why don't blind people go skydiving?

It scares the shit out of the dogs!

Two Martians crash on earth and walk to a deserted gas station. One Martian says, "This pump is mean. Let me deal with the gas station" and he shoots the pump and the whole gas station explodes. The other Martian asks how did he know that the pump was so mean.

The other Martian replies, "Anything with its dick wrapped around it once and shoved in its ear has got to be mean!"

Why did Helen Keller use two hands to masturbate?

One to do it and one to moan!

How do you know when an elephant has been fucking in your garage?

Your hefty bags are missing!

You know a bartender is pissed off when you find a string in your Bloody Mary!

What's the hardest thing about a sex change from a man to woman?

Inserting the anchovies!

Why did the guy trade his wife for an outhouse?

Because the hole was smaller and the smell was better!

Where do you get virgin wool?

From ugly sheep!

What did Adam say to Eve?

Stand back—I don't know how big this thing gets!

Did you hear about the deaf gynecologist?

He had to learn to read lips!

Why are chickens so ugly?

You'd be ugly too, if you had a pecker hanging out of your forehead!

What do you have when you are up to your ankles in blacks?

Afro-turf!

What do you say to a one legged hitchhiker?

Hop in!

What do you do with a dog that doesn't have any legs?

Take him for a drag!

Why is there a string at the end of the tampon?

So you can floss after you eat!

What's the brown stuff between elephants' toes?

Slow natives!

Did you hear about the new Helen Keller dolls?

You wind them up and they walk into walls!

What's better than roses on your piano?

Tulips on your organ.

One ovary says to the other ovary, "Hey, did you order any furniture?"
The other says, "No, why?"
"There's a couple of nuts trying to shove an organ in."

Did you hear what the bug said to the windshield?

"That's me all over!"

What's worse than being fucked by a dog?

Being fucked by a pit bull with AIDS.

Some ladies were meeting one day for tea, and Mrs. Peters asked Mrs. Roberts, "Where did you get such a wonderful arrangement of flowers?"
Mrs. Roberts said, "Oh, it's nothing. I get a different bouquet every other day."
"But who sends these lovely flowers to you?" asked Mrs. Peters. "Do you have a lover on the side?"
Mrs. Roberts replied, "Are you nuts? My husband gives them to me."
"So," asked Mrs. Peters, "what do you have to do for them?"

STILL JOKING OFF

Mrs. Roberts answered, "What do I have to do for them? Lie on my back with my legs in the air nearly twenty-four hours a day!"

"But why?" asked Mrs. Peters. "Haven't you got a vase?"

A man and woman were in bed, getting ready to make love. The woman directed the man, "Go ahead, put your finger in there." So the man did, and after a few minutes she said, "Put a few more in." So the man put a few fingers in, and then she requested, "Put your whole hand in." The man did this, and after a few moments the woman said, "Now put your other hand in." So the man did. Then the woman said, "Clap."

"I can't," replied the man.

So the woman said, "Tight, huh?"

Two men were on a safari in the middle of a dark African jungle. All of a sudden they were startled when a huge, ghastly wild cat jumped from a branch onto the neck of one of the men. The other gentleman screamed and said, "What is it?"

The first man said, "How should I know? You're the furrier!"

These three old men are sitting on a park bench discussing their problems about defecating and urinating. The first man says, "I wish I could get up every morning at 8:30 and take a leak. But it often takes me several hours."

The second man says, "I wish I could get up every morning at 9:00 and take a good, healthy shit. But it takes me forever sometimes."

The third man says, "Every morning I take a piss at 8:30, and every morning I take a shit at 10:30. But the only problem is that I don't get up out of bed until noon!"

What do you call an anorexic with a yeast infection?

A quarter-pounder with cheese!

A little boy is playing with his trains when he exclaims, "You motherfucker, horrible, bastard creepy trains!"
His mother comes up and asks, "What are you doing?"
And the little boy replies, "It's cunts like you that keep the trains from running on time!"

Why do you put duct tape around a hamster?

So it doesn't explode when you fuck it!

A couple was recently married, and the husband had to go out of town on a business trip. He was very worried about leaving his young, highly sexual wife alone, as he thought she might be tempting to some of his male neighbors, and he also didn't want her to be without sexual satisfaction. So he bought her a big vibrator and said, "Baby, I want to give this to you in place of me when I'm away. Why don't you name it, and imagine it's part of me?" The man went on the trip, and returned a week later, and found the house in total disorder—essentially a disaster area. His wife greeted him at the door with her ears stuffed with cotton, and all of her teeth had been knocked out!

During the 1992 political campaign, what did Dan Rather and designer jeans have in common?

They're both a little hard on the bush.

Late one night Johnny had a very unusual date with him in his bedroom, and wanted to tell his friend, Alfie. So Johnny called Alfie up and said, "Alfie, it's Johnny. I've got an unbelievable woman here who has a pussy with a great voice! Listen to this...." Johnny then took the receiver and put it between the girl's legs, and, lo and behold, the pussy continued with its musical magic. Johnny said, "Well, Alf, isn't that fantastic?"

And Alfie said, "Fantastic? You fucking idiot, you had to wake me at five in the morning so I could hear some cunt sing!"

Albert and Chuck were sitting in a local tavern, talking about the worst thing they had ever heard. Albert said, "I was driving along one day when I became part of a massive six-car pile-up, and all of the cars crunched together. That was absolutely the worst thing I ever heard."

Chuck said, "Well, that's bad, but the worst thing I ever heard was about ten years ago. I was in this married woman's apartment, and she was definitely a dynamite fuck. I was screwing the shit out of her, we were yelling and screaming, and all of a sudden there was a brief silence. Then I heard a key turning in the front door of the house. I knew right away it had to be her husband. I jumped up and started to dress, but her husband rushed in and grabbed me right by the balls." Albert said, "Was the worst thing you ever heard the key, letting you know you were caught?"

"No," said Chuck. "That was nothing. The worst thing I ever heard was the sound of the husband opening his penknife with his teeth!"

You know you're getting older ... when going out to a party doesn't necessarily mean you awaken with your head in the toilet.

What's it called when a bank guard takes a shit?

A security deposit!

Do you know how you define "endless love"?

Two blind people playing tennis.

What is a good barometer to use to ascertain if it is too cold outside?

Go out the night before and see if your dog sticks to the fire hydrant!

Amanda is talking to her fourteen-year-old girlfriend, Elizabeth, and says, "You know what the grossest thing that ever happened to me was?"

Elizabeth replied, "No, what was that?"

"I was sitting on my grandfather's lap and he got a hard-on!"

Isn't it amazing that they had computers way back in the time of Adam and Eve?

Eve had an Apple, and Adam had a Wang!

How do you make a tissue dance?

Just blow a little boogie into it!

Do you know the difference between an improperly knotted tie and a hunchback?

You can straighten the tie!

What do you call an unfortunate voyeur?

A man arrested at the peek of his career!

What do you call a prostitute who doesn't have any legs?

A nightcrawler!

Why do Indians wear jockstraps!

They totem pole!

What will it take to get the Beatles back together in one place?

A few more bullets!

Two leper colonies went to war, and afterwards none of the survivors of one of the colonies could walk, because they had been defeeted!

GROSS JOKES
by Julius Alvin

AWESOMELY GROSS JOKES (0-8217-3613-2, $3.50/$4.50)

AGONIZINGLY GROSS JOKES (0-8217-3648-5, $3.50/$4.50)

INTENSELY GROSS JOKES (0-8217-4168-3, $3.50/$4.50)

OUTRAGEOUSLY GROSS JOKES (0-8217-5784-9, $4.99/$6.50)

INSANELY GROSS JOKES (0-8217-5682-6, $4.99/$6.50)

BEST OF GROSS JOKES I (0-8217-5469-6, $4.99/$6.50)

BEST OF GROSS JOKES II (0-8217-5602-8, $4.99/$6.50)

THE BIG BOOK OF GROSS JOKES
(1-57566-235-3, $8.00/$13.00)

Available wherever paperbacks are sold, or order direct from the Publisher. Send cover price plus 50¢ per copy for mailing and handling to Kensington Publishing Corp., Consumer Orders, or call (toll free) 888-345-BOOK, to place your order using Mastercard or Visa. Residents of New York and Tennessee must include sales tax. DO NOT SEND CASH.

THE MYSTERIES OF MARY ROBERTS RINEHART

THE AFTER HOUSE　　　　　　(0-8217-4246-6, $3.99/$4.99)

THE CIRCULAR STAIRCASE　　(0-8217-3528-4, $3.95/$4.95)

THE DOOR　　　　　　　　　　(0-8217-3526-8, $3.95/$4.95)

THE FRIGHTENED WIFE　　　　(0-8217-3494-6, $3.95/$4.95)

A LIGHT IN THE WINDOW　　　(0-8217-4021-0, $3.99/$4.99)

THE STATE VS.　　　　　　　　(0-8217-2412-6, $3.50/$4.50)
ELINOR NORTON

THE SWIMMING POOL　　　　　(0-8217-3679-5, $3.95/$4.95)

THE WALL　　　　　　　　　　(0-8217-4017-2, $3.99/$4.99)

THE WINDOW AT THE WHITE CAT
　　　　　　　　　　　　　　　(0-8217-4246-9, $3.99/$4.99)

THREE COMPLETE NOVELS: THE BAT, THE HAUNTED LADY, THE YELLOW ROOM
　　　　　　　　　　　　　　　(0-8217-114-4, $13.00/$16.00)

Available wherever paperbacks are sold, or order direct from the Publisher. Send cover price plus 50¢ per copy for mailing and handling to Kensington Publishing Corp., Consumer Orders, or call (toll free) 888-345-BOOK, to place your order using Mastercard or Visa. Residents of New York and Tennessee must include sales tax. DO NOT SEND CASH.

Did you miss one?
Now you can buy these suspenseful books From your favorite mystery authors…

__**Baseball Cat** by Garrison Allan	1-57566-309-0/	$5.99
__**Underdog** by Laurien Berensen	1-57566-108-X/	$4.99
__**Twister** by Barbara Block	1-57566-062-8/	$4.99
__**Dead Men Don't Dance** by Margaret Chittenden	1-57566-318-X/	$5.99
__**Dead in the Water** by Connie Fedderson	0-8217-5244-8/	$4.99
__**Murder Among Neighbors** by Jonnie Jacobs	0-8217-275-2/	$5.99
__**Country Comes To Town** by Toni L. P. Kelner	1-57566-244-2/	$5.99
__**Just Desserts** by G. A. McKevett	1-57566-037-7/	$4.99
__**Tippy-Toe Murder** by Leslie Meier	1-57566-099-7/	$4.99
__**Flesh and Stone** by Mark Miano	1-57566-273-6/	$5.99
__**The Album** by Mary Roberts Reinhart	1-57566-280-9/	$5.99
__**Hunting A Detroit Tiger** by Troy Soos	1-57566-291-4/	$5.99

Call toll free **1-888-345-BOOK** to order by phone or use this coupon to order by mail.

Name_____
Address _____
City_____ State _____ Zip_____
Please send me the books I have checked above.

I am enclosing	$_____
Plus postage and handling*	$_____
Sales tax (where applicable)	$_____
Total amount enclosed	$_____

*Add $2.50 for the first book and $.50 for each additional book.
Send check or money order (no cash or CODs) to:
Kensington Publishing Corp., 850 Third Avenue, New York, NY 10022
Prices and numbers subject to change without notice. Valid only in the U.S.
All orders subject to availability.
Check out our web site at **www.kensingtonbooks.com**